WINDY DAY AT KABEKONA

Other Books by Thomas R. Smith

POETRY

The Glory 2015
The Foot of the Rainbow 2010
Waking Before Dawn 2007
Winter Hours 2005
The Dark Indigo Current 2000
Horse of Earth 1994
Keeping the Star 1988

CHAPBOOKS

Dream Union: Poems in Defense of Democracy 2014
The Night We Saved the Beatles 2012
Wisconsin Spring 2011
Kinnickinnic 2008
Peace Vigil: Poems for an Election Year (and After) 2004
North Country 2001
The Lost Music 1996

EDITED WORKS

Airmail: The Letters of Robert Bly and Tomas Tranströmer 2013
Robert Bly in This World (with James P. Lenfestey) 2011
What Happened When He Went to the Store for Bread: Poems by Alden Nowlan 1993
Walking Swiftly: Writings and Images on the Occasion of Robert's Bly's 65th Birthday 1992

WINDY DAY AT KABEKONA

New & Selected Prose Poems

1978-2018

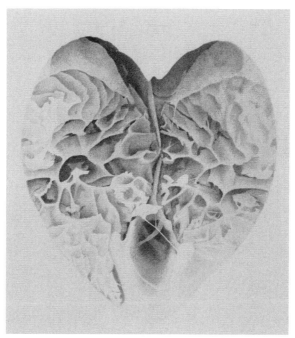

Thomas R. Smith

WHITE PINE PRESS / BUFFALO, NEW YORK

White Pine Press
P.O. Box 236
Buffalo, NY 14201
www.whitepine.org

Publication of this book was made possible, in part, by public funds from the New York State Council on the Arts, a State Agency.

Cover Art: "ad corraccoon" by Gendron Jensen. 68" x 72", graphite pencil, 1969, from *The Series on Resurrection in Nature*.

Printed and bound in the United States of America.

Library of Congress Control Number: 2017956279

ISBN 978-1-945680-18-2

Contents

INTRODUCTION

The Prose Poem: A Practice / 11

I. WHO IS THE BLIND GIRL? (1978-1988)

Killing Frost / 19
John F. Kennedy at the N-Joy Restaurant, Cornell, Wisconsin 1960 / 20
Eyes / 21
The Great Wall / 22
Waiting Room, St. Mary's / 23
Ezekiel / 24
Portrait of My German Grandparents, 1952 / 25
Sails on Lake Michigan / 26

II. CONDUCTING THE TURBULENCE (1989-2000)

The Soprano / 29
The Demolished Anthill / 30
Maple Seeds / 31
The Water Tank / 32
Praying Mantis / 33
End of Summer / 34
At the Start of the Gulf War / 35
Indian Graves on Madeline Island / 36
Small Town During a Popular War / 37
Windy Day at Kabekona / 38
The Road from Genghis Khan / 39
On the Road to New Orleans / 40
Breadcrumbs / 41
In My Parents' House at Christmas / 42

Grain Elevators / 43
On a City Bus / 44
A Sale / 45
From the Franklin Avenue Bridge in May / 46
"Aunt" Lucy / 47
Blood and Gold / 48
Snow Sticking to the Hood / 50

III. THE NEW CREATURE (2001-2009)

Your Inner Face / 53
The Forest Floor / 54
Noon on the Kinnickinnic / 55
Raccoon / 56
Hard Rock Farmers / 57
Isaac Stern Plays Dvorak's Romance in F Minor / 58
Jesus and Mary, 1978 / 59
Approaching a City by Air / 60
Mouse / 61
Rice Lake Burial Mounds / 62
Haibun: The Spell / 63
October Haibun / 64
Haibun: The Death of Tiny Tim / 65
The Crate / 66
Firewood / 67
The Green Caterpillar / 68
Brothers on the 16 Bus / 69
Breakfast in Ghent / 70
First Guitar / 72
The World We Live In / 73
A May Afternoon on the River / 74
Dream on My Birthday in January / 75
Rain at the Holiday Inn Express / 76

IV. EVERLAND (2004-2016)

Everland /

V. DAYLIGHT NATION (2010-2015)

Shells Inside a Shell / 95
A Gull's Feather /.96
Peter's Grill / 97
The Girl Who Sang with Leadbelly / 98
A Dream of Garrison Keillor / 99
The Suppressed Album / 100
Swimming on Labor Day / 101
Sympathy for the Wasps / 102
Breathe Together / 103
A Dead Crow / 104
River Otter / 105
Knowing Shit / 106
The Mole / 107
Martins Ferry, Ohio, 1987 / 108
Daylight Nation / 109

VI. BRUSHPILE SPARROWS (2016-2018)

Art Car / 113
This Abundance / 114
The Home-Going / 115
James Castle / 116
Irish Skies / 118
A Bench on the Grand Canal / 119
Newgrange / 120
Revisiting Dartington Estate After Eight Years / 121
Slapton Sands / 122
The Balloons / 123
A Broken Stone / 124
Brushpile Sparrows / 125

About the Author / 127

ACKNOWLEDGMENTS

Many of these poems were included in the following full-length collections. Thanks to the publishers for permission to reprint: *Keeping the Star* (New Rivers Press), *Horse of Earth* (Holy Cow! Press), *The Dark Indigo Current* (Holy Cow! Press), *Waking Before Dawn* (Red Dragonfly Press), *The Foot of the Rainbow* (Red Dragonfly Press), and *The Glory* (Red Dragonfly Press).

Thanks also to the publishers of these chapbooks for permission to reprint: *The Lost Music* (Bookpress) and *Kinnickinnic* (Parallel Press).

Several of the uncollected poems in this volume originally appeared in the following periodicals; thanks to the editors for permission to reprint: *Amethyst* (online, U.K.), *Askew, The Aurorean, Free Verse, Germination* (Canada), *Main Street Rag, Natural Bridge, North Stone Review, Pemmican* (online), *Sidewalks, Volume One,* and *5 a.m.*

"Brushpile Sparrows" is included in *A Cast-Iron Aeroplane That Can Actually Fly: Commentaries from 75 American Poets on Their Prose Poetry,* edited by Peter Johnson. "On the Road to New Orleans" originally appeared on the Minnesota Men's Conference *Real Men Real Words* blog, edited by Mark Gardiner. "Sympathy for the Wasps" originally appeared in *Ekphrasis: Sister Arts 2018,* a chapbook for the related exhibit at the Phipps Center for the Arts, Hudson, Wisconsin, curated by Lee Kisling, Lana Sjoberg, and Margaret Welshons,

Special thanks to poet, editor and fellow prose poem enthusiast Allan Cooper for his support and collegiality, early and late, in and out of the pages of his journal *Germination,* and to Peter Johnson, whose *The Prose Poem: An International Journal* has done much to lift the American prose poem into public awareness. Gratitude also to Nin Andrews, Robert Bly, and Peter Johnson for their supportive words for this book, and to Gendron Jensen for his generosity and friendship.

Most grateful thanks to Robert Alexander, America's champion of the prose poem, who believed in this book; his sure editorial guidance has improved it in many ways. High gratitude also to Dennis Maloney for encouragement and support along the path and for bringing this book into the distinguished company of other White Pine Press publications. Thanks to Elaine LaMattina for careful attention to the elegant design of this book. Personal thanks to publishers who took a chance on the collections in which some of these poems originally appeared, the late Bill Truesdale, Jim Perlman, and Scott King. Unending gratitude and love to Krista Spieler, my first and best reader.

For Robert and Ruth Bly
and William and Nancy Booth

and the days of Cry of the Loon Lodge
on Kabekona Lake

INTRODUCTION

THE PROSE POEM: A PRACTICE

Since the nineteenth century, the prose poem, due chiefly to the influence of its great progenitors, Baudelaire and Rimbaud, has played the role of enfant terrible in Western poetry. More radical than free verse, it abandons not only rhyme and meter, but the traditional poetic line itself, in favor of the paragraph. Its early French practitioners (for the prose poem as a defined medium is indelibly French) employed it to largely revolutionary or visionary ends — in Baudelaire the destruction of bourgeois illusions and in Rimbaud the inducement of hallucinatory states of consciousness. In the twentieth century, René Char, Francis Ponge, and Jean Follain all carried forward — each in his unique way — the prose poem's visionary imperative as established by Baudelaire and Rimbaud.

So what exactly is prose poetry? In a famous letter, Baudelaire provides this de facto definition: "Who among us has not, in his ambitious moments, dreamed of the miracle of a poetic prose, musical without meter or rhyme, supple enough and rugged enough to adapt itself to the lyrical impulses of the soul, the undulations of the psyche, the jolts of consciousness?"

David Lehman quotes Baudelaire in the introduction to his *Great American Prose Poems: From Poe to the Present,* and supplies a more contemporary if tautological definition: "The prose poem is a poem written in prose rather than verse. On the page it can look like a paragraph or fragmented short story, but it acts like a poem. It works in sentences rather than lines. With the one exception of the line break, it can make use of all the strategies and tactics of poetry."

Louis Jenkins, an American master of the form, has written usefully of the prose poem:

> "Think of the prose rectangle as a small suitcase. One must pack carefully, only the essentials, too much and the reader won't get off the ground. Too much and the poem becomes a story, a novel, an essay or worse. We know that a sonnet has fourteen lines but the prose poem is a formal poem with unspecified limits. The trick in writing a prose poem is discovering how much is enough and how much is too much." (*Nice Fish*, unpaginated)

In his marvelously original prose poem collection *This Body Is Made of Camphor and Gopherwood*, Robert Bly articulates a tiny credo for the form:

> ". . . we often feel in a prose poem a man or woman talking not before a crowd, but in a low voice to someone he is sure is listening. Through the way the prose poem absorbs detail, it helps to heal the wound of abstraction."

Rehashed arguments over a form that should no longer be controversial quickly become tiresome. Even today, some question the legitimacy of the prose poem. Prose, yes, but not a poem. Admittedly, the form can be maddeningly elusive. Why should a given piece of writing be rendered in prose format rather than in conventional lines? When I wrote my first prose poems in 1978 I had come to feel some problem with the very linearity of free verse. It seemed to me that many important experiences weren't readily accessible to the sequencing mind that struggles to make narrative sense of experience or consciousness. In the prose poem, by contrast, one could throw several elements into the air and, like a juggler, keep them there, circulating simultaneously within the paragraph. Dispensing with the poetic line also dispensed with some assumed sequentiality, allowing the simultaneous to manifest in the poem. I tried to arrange my fledgling prose poems so that the sentence order could be shifted without damage to sense.

Of course, this ignores the medium's great potential for narrative, but then there are many different kinds of prose poems. Louis Jenkins and Nin Andrews, for example, almost universally employ narrative in their prose poems. As a beginning prose poet I was interested in some of the form's other possibilities. As the prose poems collected in this book demonstrate, I soon came to incorporate more straightforward narrative in my efforts as well.

I've come to believe that the prose poem may be defined as much by its degree of relative musicality as by its visible form on the page. Traditionally, poetry in the West has occupied some midway point on the spectrum of utterance between singing and ordinary speech. One has only to listen to recordings of W. B. Yeats to hear poetry that registers very near the singing pole on that spectrum. I've told students many times that Yeats and Johnny Cash aren't so far apart in that respect (to test this for yourself, listen to Yeats reciting "The Lake Isle of Innisfree" and Cash singing "I Still Miss Someone" back to back). Practically speaking, this means that many poems occupy a middle zone on that scale of musicality, from which they could conceivably edge to one side or the other as free verse or prose poem.

But we have no objective scale for judging such matters. Yeats's style of recitation falls foreign on modern ears. We're generally accustomed to a post-Williams plain-spokenness that renders the older, more overtly musical delivery stilted and quaint to our hearing. It's probably safe to say that if Yeats registers at a position of 8 or 9 on a musicality scale of 10, then the average prose poem registers somewhere between 1 and 3. This isn't to argue that the musical content of every prose poem is the same or that the prose poem is lacking in music. In *This Journey*, for example, James Wright mischievously disguised a fully rhyming iambic pentameter sonnet, "May Morning," as a prose poem, perhaps to test the awakeness of readers, and in any case, to quote Lehman, truly "[making] use of all the strategies and tactics of poetry" save the line break. (For this revelation, I'm indebted to Kevin Stein's essay in *The Kenyon Review*, "These Drafts and Castoffs: Mapping James Wright.")

Although the vast majority of prose poems do not employ rhyme or meter of any kind, much rich sound work can still take place within those print rectangles. The ability to analyze relative musical content can help poets arrive at appropriate form for their poem. Oftentimes I've seen my own poems in that ambiguous middle zone on the scale slip from lined verse to prose poem or vice versa, and maybe back again.

Over the years my earlier mildly surreal, image-heavy prose poems have gradually given way to poems of landscape, character portraiture, and description of natural phenomena. Prose poems can obviously accommodate narrative. They are also ideal for tracking the movement of thought, and therefore especially lend themselves to the exploration of ideas and themes.

A handful of the poems in this book cross into the territory of the Japanese *haibun*, a hybrid prose-verse form most famously practiced by the haiku master Basho in the seventeenth century. One can variously conceptualize the *haibun* as prose enriched by verse or verse augmented by prose. Gary Snyder includes a few *haibun* in his collection *Danger on Peaks*, but for the most part the *haibun* is still an open frontier for American poets, as the prose poem itself was forty years ago, inviting fresh adventuring.

It must be noted that the American prose poem is not what it was in the 1970s when Robert Bly and other proponents of the so-called "deep image" set the prose poem's sometimes dark, often ecstatic, intensely psychological tone of that decade. In recent times, a paradoxical combination of lightness and density has crept into the prose poem.

As with other period poems, the prose poem becomes a vehicle for bravura voice performance while skirting the depths and heights to which the classic prose poem aspired. Many recent examples succumb to superficiality, abstraction, attitude, randomness, fragmentation, trashiness, and self-indulgent cuteness. Many starkly lack the pleasures Donald Hall has associated with the "sensuous body" of the poem. Too often these tediously dense text blocks turn out to be cell blocks to which the reader is "sentenced" for the duration of the poem. Angular masses of print sitting stolidly on the page like concrete blocks can visually repel readers' attempts to enter them. Poets can let some air into the prose poem by resisting the urge to cram everything into a single monolithic paragraph.

Though some consider the prose poem an evolutionary step forward in the development of Western poetry, I'm unconvinced by their argument. David Lehman has said, "Writing in prose you give up much. . . . The prose poem can feel like a holiday from the rigors of verse. . . ." Still, it's clear that, despite its limitations, the prose poem has proven valuable in opening up ranges of expression not previously accessible by way of the conventional free verse poem. We benefit from having varied formal choices at our disposal, and the prose poem has become a versatile strategy in the poet's tool-box of techniques.

I've included in this selection prose poems from almost all of my published books, starting with my first, in 1988, *Keeping the Star.* Many others are more recent and/or previously uncollected. The roughly chronological structure maps out some of the more recurrent locations of a life in progress.

I trust that these poems in their variety add up to something coherent, if only the record of a practice developed and maintained over nearly four decades. I am grateful to the masters of the prose poem mentioned in this introduction, and to others whom I have not mentioned, for inspiration and the challenge of this literarily amphibious form. I count myself fortunate to have come of age as a poet in a region of the country claiming such masters of the prose poem as Robert Bly, Louis Jenkins, and Tom Hennen. Behind the prose poem always I feel the salutory, restless pressure of Baudelaire and Rimbaud who, by smashing the formal barriers of their historical moment, hoped to break through to a higher visionary reality. Whether they ultimately succeeded or failed in their project, the bar they have set remains high; that may explain some of the disappointment we feel when the contemporary prose poem aims too low. In my own efforts, I have tried to be faithful to their spirit.

I. WHO IS THE BLIND GIRL?

1978-1988

KILLING FROST

The killing frost takes no prisoners. The battle of October is lost in a few hours. Soldiers occupy the village — there are stabbings in windowboxes, sudden death in the leaves. A white silhouette displaces the basil in the widow's garden. Every night a shadow grows in the cold half of her bed. She wakes before dawn to windows full of white hair.

JOHN F. KENNEDY AT THE N-JOY RESTAURANT, CORNELL, WISCONSIN, 1960

A matronly woman in a print apron is shaking the candidate's hand. She is the owner of the N-Joy Restaurant on Highway 27 where the Kennedy entourage has stopped for coffee. Her face, plump and light as a dinner roll, has risen to become the People. She is a blade of young corn moist with dew and also the cornfield, mother and daughter at the same time. He is the one who makes her so many. We do not see the Senator's eyes as the portly woman sees them, a little down-cast, the lids heavy, a softness in his gaze. He seems oblivious of his shadow on the plastic curtain decorated with pine trees.

EYES

Shadows topple through the streets as if buildings were falling. Trucks and delivery vans roll over the wishes of the dead. Rusted plow blades flop over in the graves. There is enough left alive in the slain deer's skull to die again. Campfires are seen in the windows of office complexes. Who is the blind girl no one stops for at the intersection? They drive through her, leaving faint marks on her yellow dress. Her face is a white candle. Pressed flowers fall from her mouth. She was born in a bare room, and then walked out one morning in winter, her tears breaking on the pavement like glass birds. No one sees her: There is someone she will never marry.

THE GREAT WALL

The mad are always dying, always burning, always drowning. They are already half-consumed when we meet them for the first time, the other half is being torn away. That's why, when she lifts her cup with a perfectly steady hand, sips her coffee and stares at the window, she is sitting in an electric chair, her head and armpits about to burst into flames. The mad are solid forests. The Great Wall is kept up for only a mile or two on either side of the highway. At the end of the tourists' walk, the Wall is falling apart. Snow begins to cover the sign that tells us to go no farther.

WAITING ROOM, ST. MARY'S

At 3:30 Sister Philothea rolls away the coffee tray, the time the Unit is opened to visitors. Dusk is falling over scenes on thousand-piece jigsaw puzzles. November light ebbs from the slender feet of Jesus. He is floating up, a drop of chrome on the waves.

An elderly farm couple from South Dakota have waited here since early morning for a daughter in surgery. The clothes holding them upright remember being pressed in another age. They lean forward, planting themselves in their earth of hours. The mother's hands would like to remove her heavy face and put it down somewhere for a while. Mouth tight, the man squints narrowly into the hospital's distance, driving his tractor down a long field.

EZEKIEL

The days close on golden hinges, the nights open wide; we live in a clown's accordion. There is more than one harvest, more than one moon: I saw them again in the storage room you'd sealed for the winter. Hovering, lit with faces of yellow milk, dark moths for eyes. They were the Japanese cousins of our playtime. Always there in that soft corner, shedding light on the hair of Jesus. No one else brought them. The angels were far away, waiting for us to walk in space. This morning I found a handful of bright feathers in my bootprint.

PORTRAIT OF MY GERMAN GRANDPARENTS, 1952

I see them always in midsummer, the retired minister and his
wife seated before the house too small for their thirteen children.
My grandfather lifts his feathered head, as Red Cedar River breezes
stir his few locks. His decorum and poverty show in the black wool
suit he wears even in this heat; his collar is thin but freshly bleached.
He seems to listen to a quarreling in the trees, the petulance,
perhaps, of angels thrown down. He hardly knows this world
anymore, and will not know the world it is becoming, just as the
grandchildren, grown up, will not be known. The grass, so
lantern-like on its sun-side, casts long afternoon shadows. He raises
his spotted hand to my grandmother's cheek. Her brow shines as the
sun breaks through the shade and washes the silver braids pinned up.
She is still robust, after all the comings and goings. But her old legs
are tired, folded under the rayon dress. She puts her thicker hand on
his and holds it there, feeling the slow winter pulse.

SAILS ON LAKE MICHIGAN

The sails on the horizon are neither past nor future. Journeys must be named. And that which is not a journey is a message — a triangular stamp, a scrap of linen. The wind carries flakes of bone and rice, a whiteness seen by the blood. Low waves growl up to shore, spilling their silver on the poor. Our lives are an old ring, still shining where the black is scraped away.

II. CONDUCTING THE TURBULENCE
1989-2000

THE SOPRANO

The conductor brings up violins behind the heavy-breasted woman. Tonight she is singing *Four Last Songs* by Strauss. Her knees bend, she lists to one side like a boat on the Rhine.

Notes stream upward, almost inaudibly, a breeze stirring among oak leaves or the sounds river ice makes in early spring. Suddenly what was listened for so carefully is loose in air, a passion declared after years of concealment, a storm arriving on a clear day. In a valley, sunlight flees the ripened clusters of grapes. So many not tasted, paintings never seen, cities that waited for us and we did not come. . . .

The audience feels fear beneath the intoxicating melody. In the voice's distillation is a summing up, a precise accounting of its existence, a rose fully open in this room. The hearer glimpses not only the strength and subtlety of the soul, but its dark seams also, niches of character, dislocations and failings. How difficult it is to be a woman, the grief of the new life turning in her earthen body. And then — how difficult it is to be human. The man is inside the woman and the woman inside the man, and they have never met.

THE DEMOLISHED ANTHILL

For Allan Cooper

A disaster has burst the sod and turf container of this ant town under the low-hanging shed of pines. Probably the anthill owes its devastation to a black bear foraging these Fundy woods in springtime, ripping up its living commons by the pawful.

The dome, coarse and bulging, caves slowly forward to an empty face, the eyes and nose clawed away by some savagery in the economic system. The ruin is framed by a mat of tasseled gray grass resembling wheat or hops, the beard of Dionysus in dismemberment.

It is difficult to imagine any regeneration for this exploded mound after the further attrition of rain. The few citizens still occupying its wounded labyrinth live in seclusion, although now and then one motors over a pine-needle-choked dirt road, a ninety-year-old man driving his pickup truck despite near-blindness. . . .

Alma, New Brunswick, May 1989

MAPLE SEEDS

They twirl down in May wind, heavy noses aimed at earth. Their job is to pierce like tiny darts, slice through leaves to reach their target, blunt fins upended in grass.

Most fail, but their failing helps a few succeed. The maple race goes on. Both are the tree: the gigantic wooden structure each downed flyer knows how to build, and also this community of desire scattered in the shade.

THE WATER TANK

Walking near the barbed wire fences of the cemetery, I notice wild roses twining on the strands. Their watery pink petals have wilted in the midday heat. Green flames of corn on hillsides reach toward the June sun.

I cut half a dozen of the rose stems with a pocketknife. By a southward-facing row of pines, a galvanized stock tank holds stagnant pump water. Sun and pine shade dapple the dusty rim. Film lies on the surface; two plastic milk jugs drift, half-sunk; a scrap of tinfoil crumples the light. I bend to dip the roses' stems in the lukewarm water with its wrinkled skin of dust.

What at first I took for a layer of black silt across the bottom turns out to be a bed of mosquito larvae. Seen up close, the whole mass wriggles like a thousand-fingered black rubber glove. Each larva body bends like a pulled bow, then jerks taut to move a little farther in the water.

So many we love have already vanished where these tiny archers aim in feebleness and squalor, into the horizon between the two dates carved on stone! On one of the gravestones, a large hand receiving a small hand expresses confidence in an old promise.

PRAYING MANTIS

Eye-level with the low theater of the yard, I watched the green invader with eyes luminous and gaseous as suns. It scissored above the grass's raised spears, jerky as a stop-action model, menaced with the hanging sickles of its claws, then swiveled on its turret and vanished into the high thistles.

Summer would never be so long and low and broad a stage again, although I still taste the sour wonderment of that fleeting samurai presence when I descend from my adult elevation to cling to earth's breathing fur, and wish for that tiny monster's matinee return.

END OF SUMMER

I.

September rain slants into the heavy alfalfa. Water pours from
the square and brutish mouth of the spout and runs away into the
boyish grass. Circles of rust at the bottom of the bucket are
thoughts, growing inward, of a mind simplified by solitude,
monotony of rain. . . .

2.

Things done or not done for a long time lodge in odors, in old
clothes furrowed with brooding, in black cooking-soot on the
widower's stove, in the small varnished cross nailed on a bedroom
door, and in the dirty rose curtain on tarnished brass rings — all
left as they were when the old man died.

3.

Did he paint so as not to watch night shamble toward the barns?
On the back of his cornfield scene with pheasants, we find a far
older landscape of lacquered trees and rocks. Implacably symmetrical,
halved precisely by the glass knife of a falls, the left side is green, the
right side ochre, this picture turned toward the wall.

AT THE START OF THE GULF WAR

At the corner convenience store, I write a check and can't find the date. Even the year has vanished! It has to do with the way the war is being reported — the bomb cargoes gone and "assets" in their place, the civilian casualties "collateral damage" . . . .

Has someone bombed our memory? This must be the Stone Age, and no one has yet thought of the names of the Roman gods, no one has thought of Rome. There is an empire far more ancient we are seeing now, empire of strewn boulders, of bones picked clean by leathery birds circling.

There is a sadness in the regressed streets, of words lost, things unable to speak or be spoken of. I carry the groceries and newspaper to my car; suddenly it resembles an altar of rocks used for human sacrifice. Sleet sifts before the snow-encrusted tires bearing down like mill wheels driven by some unstoppable force.

INDIAN GRAVES ON MADELINE ISLAND

For Gerald Vizenor

Despite our having known of it, we're startled to come upon this tract beyond the shops of La Pointe. Labor Day, the last wave of tourism before mist and finally frozen Lake Superior enclose the island. Masts of yachts weave above the broken pickets and uncut grass, the dusty trees and boulders. Dirt paths are worn between graves marked with either an illegible wafer of white marble or a weathered grave house. A cross of twigs lashed with yellow grass leans against each marker.

Gulls flail in wind, and know nothing of the scarcities we invent for ourselves, for others. Their cries make us desperate to live, to outlive those who died within view of the red cliffs of the mainland. Linda Cadotte at 40 laid her name here among her people's names in 1981. Lines by Edna St. Vincent Millay on her solitary modern stone rebuke the tall money of the marina:

> SAFE UPON THE SOLID ROCK THE
> UGLY HOUSES STAND
> COME AND SEE MY SHINING PALACE
> BUILT UPON THE SAND

Come and see the beautiful shacks in the weeds, doors and windows thrown open to the other world. Wood shingles stumble downward with finality, a story ending in betrayal and drunkenness, in the teller weeping. These houses aren't for staying, but are roads Ojibway souls followed for four days, nourished on wild rice, maple sugar and the wishes of the living, leaving behind in concealed drawers in the plain pine-board structures only shadows and silence.

. . .

On a corner of the highway, a post office, restaurant, and grocery store huddle together, each a cinderblock bunker in the long siege called America. A banner on the grocer's facade announces in six-inch letters names of a dozen who have enlisted in the fighting. There must be one like it in every tiny village in the country.

A lone high school student in a Metallica T-shirt loiters in the park, a clearing edged with burnt brush by the lake shore. Strange to think of leaving these springtime woods and lakes to bomb a foreign desert. . . . Such towns as these are full of desperate men and women looking for a way out of their lives. FOR SALE signs remain on some houses all year. Grass grows untended in the cemetery.

This far north, summer is a legend. The birches are indifferent to human longing; they think constantly of snow. The squirrel on a budding branch wraps its tail around the sun. We are losing the battle with winter, although the people here before us knew how to warm their dark skins without the aid of petrochemicals.

Only a picture window stands between us and the full force of gusts that lift the branches of the red pine. Drafts under the cabin door roll the rug resolutely into a tube despite our attempts to spread it flat.

Foot-high waves spume across the lake; near shore the color of the long, gleaming swells softens to a milky jade, warmer looking than it is, almost southern. But the drift of this world is northerly; lawn chairs are hurled into woodpiles, propellers of outboard motors scrape against stones. The door bangs loosely in its sill. Jackpines groan as if they could snap and fall.

There is something in all this fury that makes the day oceanic: We're near at any moment being swamped, drowned, pinned by wreckage. In the cloudless sky, the sun gleefully conducts the turbulence as though it were Wagnerian opera. A gull white as our idea of angels hovers above the shore for a moment — fully awake — fighting the wind before being torn from its place.

THE ROAD FROM GENGHIS KHAN

A copper kettle steams, makeshift humidifier, on the encrusted gas stove. Electrician's tape zigzags across a cracked window. The gas heater rumbles its low, dutiful cadence, dull-witted conversation heard through a thick wall. The rugs are grimy scraps, and a deep, bitter odor of onions pervades the narrow bunks.

Stumbling out in unlaced boots, I piss, sense around me for miles the magnificence of the snow-covered lake revolving under the stars. . . . Over breakfast, I tear from my hook a perch too small to keep, my only catch, scaly tube all mouth and muscle too dazed to find its way back down the glass-walled hole to home.

No one else in the ice-fishing shack has had better luck. Disgusted, we throw the unused minnows on the snow. I glance briefly at their pitiful flipping, then away, toward the western shore where Sunday morning traffic passes on the highway to the churches and the casino.

Once we threw other human beings on the ice to die, maybe died ourselves. . . . What a long road we're on from the bloody claws, the flayed snout, the hook passed underneath the ribs . . . the road from Genghis Khan where any refusal of cruelty is movement. . . . The sun noses its red ball up onto the ice from the waters below. The calm colors that disperse across the eastern sky still say a kingdom of kind hands could come. . . .

Fifteen hours out from Minneapolis, Jim Miller and I stand at the counter in a neon service plaza near Senatobia, Mississippi. It's a rainy Sunday morning. I've newly crossed the divide of fifty. Jim is four years out in front of me. Both of us feel every minute of our age after an all-night drive in a van with six other men. Now, having splashed our faces to a semblance of waking in the restroom, our rumpled unshavenness is on display to the politely-dressed after-church crowd, and more embarrassingly to the teenage girl with pale blond hair and beaded choker at the cash register. Before either Jim or I can complete a sentence, she chirps, "So what brings you-all this far south?" "Mardi Gras," we lie in unison, that requiring so much less explanation than a "mythopoetic" men's conference. "I should have known! Why, you-all look like a couple of party animals!" Jim grins through his grizzled beard and I through salt-and-pepper stubble, well knowing that the only kind of animal we could reasonably claim to resemble after our night in the van is road-kill possum. Still, the compliment has staying power. All the rest of that day I think of the girl, young enough to be a southern granddaughter to either of us, and of how, with an indulgent joke, she unzipped the husk of middle years from two rarin'-to-go boys on a rocky Sunday morning on the road to rocking New Orleans.

BREADCRUMBS

What do we really know of them, those fragments of the loaf that, despite their best efforts to shine in winter sunlight, in the end seem only a display of squalor to be pummeled by the fists of a broom into the sordid gutter of a dustpan? A breadcrumb can never regain the paradise of the loaf, yet neither can the loaf's purpose be accomplished without its being broken, separated from itself by that cutting or tearing with knife, hands, and teeth that hastens bread into useful states of division. To us, who have only from a distance of scale glimpsed the interior magma of spun gluten, a breadcrumb is a bridge to nowhere, or a cavern in air. But what is a breadcrumb to itself, or to God? On a winter afternoon, a breadcrumb throws a shadow many times its own size in the slant rays on a kitchen floor. .
. .

IN MY PARENTS' HOUSE AT CHRISTMAS

Opening a notebook left in the car all day, I feel how easily one could die here. The side of my pen-hand grows numb quickly as the paper draws its heat. Each unopened page is a stone hungry for warmth in the year-end darkness. No one writes long poems in the book of winter — lines freeze up, young metal becomes gray-bearded, night seals the ice fisherman's holes. Soon the cold, if we had to live in it as the trees do, would reduce the hand to immobility, dumbness.

And if I had had to go on living in this town, between the paper mill and taverns? The subzero temperature flattens clouds over pastures. The sun unicycles among black trees and slides down. The low light in the spreading pine boughs thatches a village where we would soon stiffen.

Deer kneel on the soft beds of needles sheltered from wind. Their bellies have learned to gather the fire of earth which icy rivers of air pour over. The pine needles care about light as we care about heat, the conditions of their life having made them a little crazy, like Taoists.

GRAIN ELEVATORS

The sky opens a golden vein at sunset. We cut sunflowers and daisies from the railroad's fugitive gardens. I wipe the sticky blood of summer on my trousers.

We love walking in the shadows of those giants — strange architectures, functional yet in flight, colossi conjured from gravel pits and mines and from our hunger for bread.

Corrugated houses perch on concrete cylinders. One old tarred tower with Mondrian windows resembles from afar a night-lit skyscraper collaged against the pale blue afternoon.

We admire a shed calmly pitched atop the highest silo — pigeons flutter from the broken panes, our other life kept safe there, above the boxcars' loading and unloading, yellow and heavy with seed and inclined toward the sun.

The little Iranian scrunches down, squirming with laughter at what the dopey-sounding American in the baseball cap seated in front of him is saying: "This ain't like Eye-ran, buddy. We don't have any of them Commonists here." Possibly the foreigner is half-crazy. Or maybe he finds the thick-tongued American hysterically funny. Or both. For his part, the American, though evidently considering himself the foreigner's better, appears pleased to receive this attention, however peculiar.

Nearing his stop, the American adjusts his cap, holds out a meaty fist at which the Iranian merely stares. "Tell ya what, pal," he says. "You better chill out."

Beneath his nest of mad curls, the foreigner pulls himself up, grasps the seat-back with livid fingers. He is sweating, his face raspberry-red. His head is a champagne cork about to pop. *"Sheel out? What is SHEEL OUT?!"*

The American smiles sadly. "Listen to me, buddy. You better chill out right now, or they'll throw ya in the slammer." The bus has stopped. He stands up and, without looking back, exits.

It is December. Snow flattens everything outside the fogged windows. Two women watching across the aisle exchange private looks. Tears of laughter stream from the corners of the Iranian's eyes.

A SALE

Things look altered, individual, in sunlight — a book with a red cover or a green glass vase, a copper canister, dining room chair, or paperweight, its identity reclaimed from the indiscriminate mass.

Last month the second of two hoarder sisters in their nineties went into the nursing home. Room after room of piles and boxes . . . entire shelves of irons and toasters . . . enough faux pearls to outfit an army of Miss Havishams . . . kitchen utensils sufficient to serve a convent . . . hats, towels, gloves, clocks, jello molds, scarves, purses, screwdrivers, fans. . . .

A heavy woman with steel-colored curls collects quarters from a man in a red plaid jacket. A month-old infant with fine black hair dozes at her hip. The hard-eyed woman affirms that treasures have been unearthed here, though at some cost of effort and stomach. She grimaces: "A real digger-puker."

The dim, muffled rooms warehouse petty objects that somehow add up to lack rather than abundance. One imagines the sisters, their isolation and acquisitiveness taken concrete form, startled now and then into awareness of that wave of unredeemed matter they've become powerless to control, rising suddenly to tow them under, then that awareness itself pulled down. . . .

Leaning from the rail, I see in the currents how much spring costs the Mississippi in uncertainty and turmoil — eddies fed by melted snow stir the bottom, a brown stew that boils up suddenly. Thinnings in the clouds cast reflective nimbuses on the swirled coppery metalwork of the river. A railroad trestle's double lies down like a ladder into deep water.

Moist, shadowless air flattens the prospect without haziness, a thin veil interposed between the world and our vision, that tenderness without which, as Dostoevsky said, truth is unjust.

A daylight phosphorescence fountains from lemony willows, feathery stoles of cottonwoods and elms, even the ground itself — fallen trunks and secretive folds of dunes, every rock and twig that took the hit of winter, all climb to meet the sun. A fine lace of earth's imagination clothes the angel in leaves and blossoms.

"AUNT" LUCY

The oldest residents of Cameron, Wisconsin remember "Aunt" Lucy St. Louis, my grandparents' next-door neighbor, who died at one hundred in the house where, in the prime of her womanhood, she'd raised her widowed brother's eight children. Some unecumenical Lutherans in my family to this day begrudge Catholics a place in heaven, yet argue an exception was surely made for Lucy, single-handedly tending that motherless brood during the time when she might have borne her own.

I stood often with my cousins before a chicken-wire cage where Lucy's talking crow, magnetic in its shiny blackness, tirelessly croaked its name, "Joe! Joe! Joe!" When lectured by my righteous grandfather for cruelly imprisoning a wild creature, Lucy, furiously gumming her pipe, retorted, "Well, what about your goldfish? They're in jail too!" after which my grandfather emptied the fishbowl in the city pond.

Lucy, "Aunt" to everyone, including her neighbors' grandchildren, claimed to have cured with herbs a cancer on her nose, God's punishment to fit the crime of her "nosiness." She outlived not only the cancer but her reason, became herself a kind of crow fluttering madly against her earthly cage, one autumn night unnerving even my sturdy old German grandmother by pressing her divinely chastened nose flat against the bedroom window.

Like my cousins and siblings, I grew up not entirely sure that Lucy wasn't the "aunt" I'd thought she was, so fundamentally did she share in the fierce, admirable, and foolish stubbornness of my mother's people.

Two days after Christmas, we're sitting, twelve at the table, in a Wisconsin banquet room dimly lit as a tavern in a Russian novel. We drove in two cars through snow-drifted dairy country, dense birch groves alternating with radiantly white fields under a mild sun and finely layered clouds. This is the sort of day, says Aunt Helen, that my parents were married.

Eight people attended the wedding — the bride and groom, both sets of parents (with Grandpa Rathke officiating), and Helen and Husky. Afterward my parents, not yet owning a car, took the train back to Eau Claire. Snapshots of the occasion suggest loneliness and unease. We pass them around the table, the children and their partners encouraging the elders to reminisce. We ask about the circumstances of the proposal, which my father says took place in a bowling alley, although my mother doesn't remember it. She's not proud of the marriage, though she takes clear satisfaction in this dinner honoring their fifty years.

Time for toasts. I imagine myself rising: "Let us drink to this couple's journey through the dark forest without a map. Much has been suffered and much lost, but we are still here, all of us alive, and none to be younger than we are tonight."

My father, leaning close, whispers hoarsely: "I know a toast, too. I'll just tell you, not the others:

> "That great moment of repose,
> Belly against belly,
> Toes against toes.
> After that great moment of delight,
> Fanny against fanny
> The rest of the night."

It's a joke, but also an inadvertent image of a marriage in which the partners have spent the past twenty-five years with their backs turned to each other. My father's new red tie and my mother's red earrings echo the red rose corsages they wear, seeming to acknowledge the blood each has drawn and shed over five decades. That blood has branched four times in their four children, three more times in grandchildren. Finally it is the blood we celebrate.

SNOW STICKING TO THE HOOD

I've driven ninety miles and still the inch-thick crust of last night's snow clings to the hood. It's like a lamb being slowly sheared, this blue-skinned beast with patchy fleece. A swath suddenly sifts loose, a climber torn by gales off Annapurna, flumphs upward against the windshield, then over the top into the slipstream, hurled God knows where in the cold sunlight.

Someone else is driving now. I look sideways, see my father at the wheel, not dead anymore, but young, with his full head of wavy hair, his aromatic cigar, his confident expression. I'm barely tall enough to see over the dashboard where high-velocity winds are flaying the snow with their knives. There's a lot of violence out in that world, but Dad's in control here. It's hard to even imagine taking his place. I'll just stay small, where the wind and snow part for him. And we'll arrive safely wherever it is we're going.

III. THE NEW CREATURE

2001-2009

YOUR INNER FACE

Like everyone, you have two faces: One of them others see, in restaurants and banks — it's only approximate, the probable cause when you feel misjudged by the world.

On the inside there's another face through which you reach toward that world: Pure gesture, it registers instantaneously each nuance of feeling, like a film star or Mother Teresa, an interior sky. When you weep, clouds darken with rain; when you laugh, all the pigeons fly up into the light.

It's this face you'd prefer to be known by, so true to its desires, unbelievably beautiful. When two people glimpse it in each other, we call that love — and if someone should see all the secret faces at once, heaven.

Early March in the woods. Half the sky is clear, half cloudy. A layer of diffuse sunlight rests over everything, lightly, as the present rests over the world of the past.

The mat of dead leaves has dried on top, but remains moist underneath, half-lifted from the damp soil. The scabrous mantle of leaf-mulch stretches, pulls loose and gradually breaks up. . . .

I'm drowsing, while under the forest's papery winter skin the earth is awakening. In exposed spaces tiny perfect stars gather their green rays. Small fires move darkly on thin legs.

Earth is trying to remove a stiff mask from her green and black face. We all know that attachment to the past and the engulfing splendor from which it shrinks. What do I hope to conceal from myself, underneath my thousands of dead leaves?

NOON ON THE KINNICKINNIC

The water gleams in glassy protuberances where the tops of submerged rocks surface. The sound they make says, "It's all right." We follow a path among lacy white flowers of April. Limestone bluffs bulk up against blue sky. Bare branches shine intricately. Every space that the shade will flood in a few weeks is still wide open and filled with light. How I love the shadows of trunks this time of year, flowing over the radiant floor of the woods. They pulse with life like the striped snake we watch pull itself in muscular S-curves broadside the swift current, its head glistening darkly, disappearing in reeds on the opposite shore.

RACCOON

Returning from my morning walk along the river, passing the culvert a second time, I suddenly see it: gray-faced animal wrapped from inside around the grate, its posture the ancient agony and submission to death. Stiff front and hind legs thrust out, the body folds around the metal bars that caught it mid-belly, snout twisted down and outward, baring the white corn of the teeth.

Our summer has been dry, followed by heavy rains. This concrete tunnel under meadows empties down from housing construction on South Main. A contained flood inside the storm sewer swept the raccoon away, slammed and pinned it here, where it died from drowning or concussion or both.

Pass by in your haste, and ignore it. Or notice the coarse-furred limbs extended, reaching for some withheld deliverance. Think of the new streets and homes, the people who no longer know where they are. Notice how closely the hands resemble your own.

HARD ROCK FARMERS

Saturday night at the tavern on the corner where the highway turns north, middle-aged bar band veterans crank deafening rock and roll from speakers stacked ten feet tall. The regulars are less interested in fighting than in tapping each other playfully on the chest pockets of their bib overalls while hoisting a Leinenkugel's Big Butt and a Marlboro, or dancing goat-like from the waist down to the band's crashing rhythms.

Their children have flown via the Internet. On the juke box, there are CDs by Mojo Nixon and Social Distortion. Lots of baseball caps, though none worn backwards.

Despite the occasional woman — say, a fine-boned, big-haired blond in a white leather jacket — this watering hole clearly belongs to the men. After a week of machinery repairs, milking, and trying to hold a world together that everyone knows is spinning out of control, they relax by taking into themselves a bit of the destructive element.

At midnight the tiny building crowded by pickup trucks and corn fields vibrates on its foundation, gathering momentum to join the exodus from earth.

Standing in his black tails, his bow lifted antenna-like, he lightly shifts his weight from one foot to the other, the fingers of his right hand clapping soundlessly against the palm.

He is already in the music; his only waiting is for the appropriate moment to speak, not loudly, but with absolute conviction. He knows where he is, and practices what I once heard a shaman call "being in a place well." He registers every note, every instrument's voice around him, every change in air, every silence, and knows that when he opens his wings, a warm, melancholy breeze will buoy him perfectly and gracefully in the desired direction.

Now he turns his face toward us, its rondure entirely absorbed in the delivery of Dvorák's bittersweet melody. He is a great old bee making honey again from the living black flowers of the score. Life is not about owning things, the music says: Disperse what is most precious into the air, a humidifying spray for dry souls.

The backdrop of black tuxedos and dresses these musicians present to the audience, against which faces and hands appear at their most animate, tells us not to be afraid of the dark. A good shadow gave and took back Dvorák, and has given and one day will take back Isaac Stern, though not their gifts to us, nor the capacity of hands to climb from black sleeves into the light and make this music.

JESUS AND MARY, 1978

They're the hardest-working panhandlers in Amsterdam: Jesus with his matted beard and Mary with her dirty blond hair dreadlocked by weather and neglect, Jesus so tall he seems twice Mary's height. Holding out sun-and-dirt-darkened palms, they look rubbery, like caterpillars rearing on a leaf. Refuse them and Jesus's grizzled scowl implodes, a black hole, and tears scald Mary's cheeks. He pulls her doll-like, so fast her feet can barely skim the ground, though a few dozen yards away the two instantly recover an intense composure midway between appeal and demand.

I fantasize for them a different life after hours because being "Jesus and Mary" looks so hard I can't imagine anyone doing it full-time. Once after midnight, beneath my friend Joop's window, a voice called from the alley. Everyone got up to look: In the moonlight, alone and as if naked because not clothed by a crowd, lanky Jesus stood with his diminutive shadow Mary. In a scene I understood had repeated often, Joop knifed from a hunk of hashish a generous brownish wedge, tossed it down to them. Fluid as a mime, Jesus caught it, and tipped an imaginary hat to his benefactor. Then with a solicitous tenderness, he took Mary's small, chapped hand and vanished with her into the fragrant May darkness.

(Joop is pronounced "yope" as to rhyme with "hope")

APPROACHING A CITY BY AIR

The land stretches flat as a road map at the bottom of an ocean of April light. A map as large as the territory. . . . The towns edge closer together, smaller cross-hatchings lying within the rule of highways.

Developments under construction are petroglyphic, a child's drawing, simplified, a place for the half-formed figures of a grade-schooler's imagination to live.

Established neighborhoods closer in to the city center complicate the texture, a sea of houses, each doing its part to stake down the planet's surface, iron out its unpredictability and passion, its flux. Swimming pools are turquoises set in a staggeringly ornate piece of jewelry.

Gray expanses of industrial and commercial rooftops glitter with veins into which the heroin of globalization has been injected. Proliferating wilderness of "free" trade! Under the Monopoly rooftops, millions of frightened hearts beating. . . .

Earth Day 2001

MOUSE

Furry gray scoop of homelessness, hunched farmwife trying to find her way among giants: The surprise of first glimpsing her on the bookstore carpet quickly turns to pity as I watch her dither and bumble, come to a stop like an upended wind-up toy spinning its wheels.

From the back room, a young woman clerk wearing on her black T-shirt a Code Pink button produces cardboard and an old aluminum pot. "We put out poison," she explains, "but I don't approve." Bending, she claps the pot over the mouse, slides the cardboard deftly under paws.

For a moment, the tail, caught, flicks feebly before the mouse pulls it in to herself. The clerk carries her outside to bushes where she can die in privacy. Only then, after a week of fury and bombing, war within the country and myself, does this small act of human kindness release my grief.

March 27, 2003, Ruminator Books, St. Paul

RICE LAKE BURIAL MOUNDS

Hot evening at the end of a day's travel. Condensation from air conditioning drips under parked cars at the rest stop. My shirt unsticks from my back as we walk in a breeze like weak tea. The path leads farther than one would expect, past the toilets and woods scrubby and littered enough to suggest illicit meetings and drug deals.

Strangely, we're walking only a few yards from the shoulder of the freeway. On our right, dust clouds from a denuded field where bulldozers scuff and rumble. Here, on the path, some large machine trampled and dragged branches, which lie crushed and green-smelling.

Just ahead are the mounds, a dozen or so feet tall, overgrown, fenced in. The plaque says that the people who built them lived between 800 and 1700, hunting, fishing, and farming around Rice Lake, which we can glimpse from this slight elevation, sparkling hazily across the freeway.

There's not much here but some leafy hillocks in the shaded quiet of a cul-de-sac surrounded by concrete and concrete-to-be. Still, a presence of some sort offers itself in the deepening shadows. To fully partake, one would have to clear away the mechanical noise and frenzy to live as the dwellers in this place once did.

Before them, I feel loss and shame, but also a twinge of awe, thinking of the old ones who've lain in these mulchy hillocks, some of them for a thousand years.

Turning back toward the car, we still hear bulldozers working overtime to scrape more land bare for houses for commuters who will buy more gasoline to operate their minivans to make more oil wars necessary. But for a moment the mounds' strength overrides all that, settles on my spirit like a memory of some glory that has left the world. An intense horizontal copper-red beads through the treeline. Where we have been, we were not alone.

HAIBUN: THE SPELL

I'm just about to leave for work, when suddenly my mother appears in the room. She looks appealingly mischievous, as though keeping some benign secret. My father now stands beside her; his grin says he's in on it, whatever it is. Both of my parents radiate good health, smartly dressed in the styles of their young adulthood in the Forties; in fact, they *are* younger, about the age they were when I was born. Relaxed and smiling, they actively enjoy each others' company, in a way I rarely witnessed when Dad was alive. Finally the spell of their marital unhappiness has lifted. . . .

Waking to the bright spring morning, I discover scraps of sadness clinging to me like dead leaves to the clothes of a person who has slept in the woods. Rising, I can't quite brush them off:

> Spokes of the sun-wheel flash through the blinds,
> beams from the projectionist's window,
> starting up once again
> the old lovelorn movie of the world.

OCTOBER HAIBUN

Each morning the trees stand more starkly, intricately exposed. I too am becoming more visible as my leaves fall. I treasure most those days when the leaves drop almost without sound, when I can hear the voice of a poem arriving above the chat and furor of the wind.

> Nights are colder.
> Realizing I can't open
> every door I pass.

Cutting back comes with autumn, abandoning what doesn't contribute to movement, unclogging the conduits that carry energy for living. Each stump cleared makes way for fresh growth. In principle, I agree. Yet looking out the window at sky the foliage once softened and brought nearer, how can I not grieve?

> I bag old or unread
> books to sell in the city.

HAIBUN: THE DEATH OF TINY TIM

Burying him in the same cemetery with Hubert Humphrey makes an odd sort of sense. Come spring, he and the Happy Warrior can go tiptoeing through the tulips together at Lakewood.

Once at a party, a woman filming a documentary on Tiny told me how on a Saturday he'd flown back to Des Moines to retrieve his ukulele from a dumpster after leaving it in a bar he'd played Friday night. I pictured him old — he claimed sixty-four, though others added a decade — grubbing among the empty beer bottles, dyed curls limp around his powdered nose.

Yet the obituaries painted him content in South Minneapolis, his last, unlikely home, with his third wife, Miss Sue. (Every woman was, to him, "Miss.") Before they closed the casket, drag queens and geezers jostled to have their photos taken with him.

The papers listed Tiny by his birth name, Herbert B. Khaury. He sang his last note at the posh Woman's Club of Minneapolis, then stepped off the stage into eternity.

> Think well of him,
> never less than gentlemanly,
> unfailingly polite until the end,
> even to old Mister Death.

THE CRATE

Made to use only once, yes, undoubtedly — all too often sighted in the trash, still perfectly good, its coarse, crisp wooden slats unmarred by delivering whatever by now has departed toward its own end.

"Wiser not to dwell too long on its fate," wrote the sapient poet. In lean days of my youth, I might salvage from a dumpster or loading dock just such a crate, clean and sound, "shabby chic," " repurposing" before its time, for a shelf to house treasured books until the next move.

Isn't the universe far more mysterious and varied than any of us knows? Don't the mystics say, "As above, so below"? Let's not dismiss the possibility that someone or something whose nature eludes us as completely as our nature eludes the wooden crate may yet, from need, desire, or even whimsical fondness, re-use us even after, having fulfilled our original purpose, we've been set out on the planetary curb for the Great Garbage Collector in the Sky.

With a bow to the spirit of Francis Ponge

FIREWOOD

Flames are taking the rough pine slab I've leaned into the fireplace kindling. The bed of embers is polymorphous — feathery, scaly, slaty, silky. Caves glow deep inside the miniature black mountain that squeaks faintly in its transports like rubbed glass.

I set to one side, in the fireplace but apart from the fire, three heavy chunks of slightly damp oak. Looking on, they begin to steam, their grainy faces combed by firelight. Not as blank as one might expect — a knothole says *O!*

The flame is not external to the wood, but instead is its essence, dancing its religion, its long tongues licking the pine board's belly and evaporating upward into the most ephemeral scarves. If asked, it would have made a roof to keep us dry for a hundred years. Above the flue and into the night, it escapes toward its homeland of stars.

THE GREEN CATERPILLAR

Leaving the checkbook on the table, I walk out of the house and down to the river. It's late afternoon, September. The trees take the lowering light that is driving the sap back down to their roots and shutting, door by door, the rooms of the leaves. A leaf, a river, they are always here, even when we don't know where the money will come from.

On the path I see a fat peapod. No, it's a green caterpillar stretching itself along. The path is a rocky, uneven gash in the earth with grass tufts on either side and granular dirt resembling brown sugar. The caterpillar appears half helpless and half purposeful, its small smooth head weaving steadily as if to get its bearings, its body bunching, a ripple running down its length as the front part hoists the rest of it forward.

It negotiates the litter of stones and leaves that must make its wayfaring a tedious if not painful proposition. At one point it loses purchase and rolls an entire revolution sideways before regaining its grip. This slippage affords me a better view of the spots on its side, irregular, yellow with black as if carefully inked with a fine brush. Now the caterpillar has fallen from the sunlight into a shaded recess — whether a good, bad or neutral development, from the caterpillar's perspective, who can say.

As I watch, something in me turns toward sympathy. When I first recognized this thumb-sized citizen of a deeply nonhuman country, my first reaction was disgust, then pity for its having to nose along so slowly on the raw, uneven ground.

But realizing there's no separation between this creature and its nature, no anxiety over how it will live, I come to admire, and almost envy, the caterpillar for the way it advances determinedly over rocks that have lodged where they are — not from any desire to thwart or obstruct but from a necessity of their own — and which the caterpillar must, without hesitation or blame, accommodate as best it can.

A man a little older than I, long-haired, maybe an aging hippie or vet, studies his paperback as we bump along the wintry street. He has the stringy look of an itinerant monk, someone who's spent his life without much worldly power, trying to stay alive and do good, or at least do no harm. When he moves to assist with a wheelchair being lifted on board at a stop, the driver, normally gratingly cheerful, snaps at him, "You leave that alone! I get paid for doing this!" The graybeard backs into his seat, wary, unchastened. Soon he's in his book again, though remaining alert.

A large shaven-headed man across the aisle makes a point of talking to the other passengers. His demeanor is rough, his complexion raw. He's between forty and fifty. He compliments a young white man wearing an African pillbox hat, "Nice hat," but the man passes silently down his private stony tunnel. The big man greets me as he steps down to exit. I reply, "Take it easy." Through the frosted window I watch him slowly tug his jacket hood over his pale, scraped head. He wears no gloves — none left behind, I check to see, on his empty seat — but shuffles along the salted city sidewalk, hands hanging red at his sides. Oh who are they, and where are they going, these brothers, men "divine as myself. . . ."

BREAKFAST IN GHENT
1992

Mist still hovers over the spindly November fields as Robert and I drive onto the main street of Ghent, Minnesota, and pull up in front of the M&M Cafe. The morning's mood so far has been minor key, the piercing, icicle-like dissonances of a Grieg piano piece. But when we step into the cafe, it's the sunburst of a Bach cantata. Or rather it is Bill Holm, the first and only customer to arrive before us, in his shirt with rolled-up sleeves and blue pinstripes, smoking a cigarette (surely not the first of the day). Technically, Bill is sitting, but there is something of the tall man's slouch in his posture, as if from any vantage he must peer downward from his tower of irrepressible spirits.

The walls of this place exude a soft glow whose source is neither the room's lighting nor the cheerfully patterned wallpaper. No, the M&M Cafe is irradiated by some other energy, perhaps the overheated molecules of the story Bill Holm is even now in the midst of telling his friends, the cafe owners Marian and Mark, and certainly by the improbably robust appearance of the deep pink face from which blue eyes identify small details, perhaps unnoticed by others but extraordinarily interesting, in nearly everything they see.

Bill holds forth on recent escapades in China: his bed full of scorpions, and furniture "just sticks," a roof leaking in twelve places; his collapse misdiagnosed as a serious heart attack in Hong Kong and eventually, back in Minneota, Minnesota, treated with aspirin, "the $1.99 Kresge's kind"; how, enraged for six weeks by the injustices of Chinese society, he figures his arteries just "constricted in sympathy" with a bound people.

Bill complains of still feeling worn down by his travel, though Robert observes that weight loss apparently isn't one of the symptoms. "I eat," Bill explains. "The mouth is open!" and he points comically to his open maw surrounded by whitening beard. His alleged brush with mortality seems not to have intimidated him, for he whips out another Merit, lights it, and exclaims that someone must preserve these incorrect habits lest the world become too boringly well-behaved. It's clear he views his vices as an endangered species, and himself as a kind of joyful bad habits preserve. It may be difficult for him to imagine life without them, but it is harder yet for us to imagine a world without Bill Holm.

FIRST GUITAR

My first guitar bore, as badge of its possibly dissipated former life, the ring a bottle might leave on a polished table top. At fourteen, I was sure it had been a beer bottle.

Bought by my father for ten dollars from a musician friend, it came strung backwards, left-handed, a practical obstacle. It's a wonder Dad even bothered to procure that scarred Stella acoustic (like Leadbelly played, though that would have meant little to me then). He loathed rock and roll, and it was my mother who smuggled the first Elvis record into our house.

The Stella's neck was so warped I could barely muster finger-strength to press strings to frets. But I was determined, and developed an iron grip to wrest basic chords from that hard-luck box.

I and three fellow acolytes of the new British sound taught ourselves and each other the songs of our chosen tribe. I saved money from my after-school newspaper job for a Hagstrom electric, but toted the Stella to the park summer evenings to serenade camper girls lured away from their parents, under conditions of suitably Troubadour-like unfulfillment.

Graduation scattered us four co-conspirators after too short a time making our joyful noise. Still the Stella stuck with me for years, the husk of a dream, from dorm to crashpad, until I thoughtlessly left it behind in a hippie farmhouse where I lived the winter the Beatles' "white album" publicly exposed their fracture.

I've regretted that casual carelessness, and wondered what became of my sturdy, resonant companion. Did it end in some attic, decayed glue releasing the high tension of its neck? Or has it docked in other ports, still delivering its cargo of romantic possibility? Does some fresh beginner even now painstakingly spell out on its raised strings the familiar truncated alphabet of desire?

In a friend's house, I reacquaint myself with the "LIFE Special Edition for Young Readers." Copyright 1956 — I was eight, just the right age for poring over Chesley Bonestell's paintings of the "wastes" of Mercury and the double star Beta Lyrae bound together by rings of crimson hydrogen. Almost every photo and illustration, memorized in minute detail, leads me into reverie these many years later. Imagine — the world we live in!

But is it? It's true that the trilobite fossil dozes on, and has not yet awakened. Cumulus clouds, composed of some of the same atoms as those in the photos, shake their electric fists at dry trees on stormy summer days.

But not a single one of the bass, squid, katydids, coyote, sea anemones, opossums, kangaroo rats, king snakes or caribou pictured in these pages is still alive. This book of dreams is also a book of the dead. Not quite the world we live in anymore, though one resembling it, a seed-world from which the present world has grown. A world the book's authors hoped the child reading would feel a part of, and maybe a little because of them, he did.

A MAY AFTERNOON ON THE RIVER

As I descend the path, the steaming caldron of new leaves radiates steady sun-heat. Rains have swollen the chocolaty river. White water races its bicycles down the overflowing dam. The current glides on, carrying away shadows left from winter.

I sit with my back against an old wardrobe willow, the roots damp, the trunk dry. Afternoon sun pours into the space between me and my book. My gaze tangles in the light whirling the brown water. The light is stopping the river in its flow, lifting it in place, spinning it into a silver cloud that hovers. . . .

Abruptly the sun yanks back its bright threads. Thunderclouds bulge over the hills on the western shore. Nimbuses of rain, far off, drive fast. Smell of crushed pine and cedar boughs. The river darkens to a muddy shadow, preoccupied and muttering. Everything is telling me, *Go*. As I climb the bank, the wind slams its doors behind me.

It's midsummer. I'm in love with a young woman from India who works in a home for elderly ladies. We meet in a park near the home. Her skin is brown against her white uniform.

I'm showing her something marvelous I've discovered. I dig deep in the thick uncut grass: It's a butterfly, or the husk of one — in the thorax, behind the wings, there's a hole from which some new creature, of which the butterfly was only an earlier stage, has emerged.

Droplets on the window multiply to a steady patter, then pelting, then liquid slabs sliding sideways against the exterior wall of the motel. Thunder like some improportionate judgment.

Lightning exposes radiant contours of the snapping sheets of rain. Downspouts pour small cataracts against the horizontal grain of the storm.

We turn out the room lights and watch the dazzle buffeting the night screen, the drama of the wind over newly planted cornfields, thin green lines scribbled incoherent by swarming pencil-tips. Rain, velocity, and darkness blur the fast food oases, gas stations brandishing the bait of freedom, the giant mouse in red lederhosen climbing the Cheese Chalet, signs along the highway reading THIS LAND AVAILABLE FOR DEVELOPMENT and FUTURE SITE OF RYAN'S FUNERAL HOME, a home that is not our home.

The slant rain overwhelms all of these, confuses them with a saving indeterminacy. Amid this violent conformity, certain particles, wet sparks, the reckless ones, somehow freer than the rest, move in other directions. . . .

IV. EVERLAND (2004-2016)

EVERLAND

The invincible shield of caring
is a weapon from the sky against being dead.
—*Lao Tzu (trans. Witter Bynner)*

Start a huge, foolish project,
like Noah.

It makes absolutely no difference
what people think.
—*Rumi (trans. Coleman Barks)*

Power on.
—*Dr. Evermor*

Invincible Shield

Early April, the land beneath rain and sun raw as our newly laid-bare feelings after winter. Driving south from Baraboo on US 12, we see to the east, close by the Wisconsin River, the decommissioned Badger Ordnance plant. West of the highway, giant metal — bugs! — gangly, brightly painted — stride the ditches. A twenty-foot-high iron heart skewered by an ornate arrow calls to mind Lao Tzu's "invincible shield of caring." We leave the car among spring-fountaining trees near a sign announcing *Dr. Evermor's Sculpture Park.*

Around the Bend

Up ahead scrap-heaps flank the dirt road, glimmer among delicate
young leaves. On the path into Dr. Evermor's populous, constructed
world, inquisitive presences press from all sides, from bushes, from
the deep, dead grass: Hundreds, maybe thousands of metal creatures
— whiskered, horned, beaked, wingèd, pincered, finned —
motionless yet quick with whimsical personality, exude no menace,
only playfulness, not an army but an eccentric village, welcoming
winter-worn travelers into the light.

Forevertron

It all radiates out from the Forevertron — four hundred tons of soaring, sprawling, baroque engineering, part carnival midway, part Victorian science fiction, part Gaudian excess, spiral-staircasing, telescoping Machine Age collage, according to Dr. Evermor's writings an earth-sky harmonizer, bad karma neutralizer, the elegant copper-encased glass egg above the Tesla coils designed to one day "perpetuate" its creator "back into the heavens."

The Doctor Is In

Near a welding station, a speaker hoisted on a pole pipes circus music. A hammer taps rhythmically nearby in April air peppery with spray paint. Drifting out past the Forevertron, constellations of sculptures all sizes: impish crab and lobster hugging the ground, dueling swordfish, flies huge as helicopters, towering birds with steel-guitar bodies. A smiling woman introduces herself as Lady Eleanor Every. "The Doctor enjoys meeting visitors. Stop and say hello!"

Fox

While Krista chats with Lady Eleanor I venture into Dr. Evermor's rusted minibus office. He's talking loudly with a younger man in coveralls. It's as though a fox has spotted me from his lair! There's an atmosphere of conspiracy, of plotting some friendly mischief for the world over a bag of chips. A cat on the sun-splashed caramel-colored seat is in on this too. "We're having a discussion," the Doctor tells me. "Sit down and shut up until we finish." He adds, "Then we'll get to *your* problem!"

Jails

Dr. Evermor looks dapper in his purple shirt and silk ascot. His golden belt buckle is shaped like a scallop shell. Deep vertical brow-furrows, a head of dark, thick hair, blunt, inquisitive nose. A life dealing in scrap has knit an ironic shrewdness above his eyes, which droop like Neruda's. What kind of doctor is he anyway? Maybe an Industrial Metaphysician? He sketches loosely in a notebook on his lap, plans to cut up some old jails he bought in Illinois. "Why jails?" "Because I *hate* jails!"

Salvage

Tom Every got his start in the scrap business at age eleven. In his forties, through with demolition, he began his monumental life's work of reclamation. Call it art or what you will, his genius for animating the cast-off and obsolete attracted attention, some of it unwanted as when pornographers attempted a photo shoot in front of the Forevertron (he ran them off). And by the way, has he mentioned that the Bird Band, built with old musical instruments, comes alive and plays on nights of the full moon?

Names

Finally the Doctor turns his curiosity toward me. "What's your name?" I tell him. "Bullshit," he snorts. That unnerves me, as if I've been caught using a fake ID. Could a name also be a kind of jail? This man salvaged his "Tom" and built from it "Dr. Evermor." And what about this "problem" of mine he's mentioned? Does he just mean that I'm past fifty, and it's springtime? The Doctor notices my abashed silence, and softens his look. He fixes kindly, sad sea-turtle eyes on me, and asks, "Are you happy?"

Heavenly Hope

During World War II, the federal government uprooted generations-old farms on prime land to build the munitions factory; some say the community never recovered. Dr. Evermor has devised a plan to heal that long-standing wound by moving the Forevertron, his monumental peace generator, across the highway to the site of Badger's old compressor plant. He's a romantic, a Parsifal with a welding torch, dreams of powering the modern-day wasteland back to bloom.

Dr. Evermor hates things that imprison imagination — like television and alcohol — and grieves the loss of craft-work in the modern world. "I think of all these" — his sweeping gesture takes in the whole of Everland — "as time-binding devices." Nineteenth-century ironwork is especially beautiful to him. He brings in semi-loads of dead farm machinery each week. He points proudly to a culvert-sized cylinder. "The aerospace industry paid a million bucks for that, but I got it for a hundred."

Salt

The Sufis tell this story: A teacher mixes a handful of salt in a jar of water and asks his student, "How does it taste?" "Bitter!" Then he throws an equal amount of salt in a lake and bids his student drink. "And how does that taste?" "Sweet!" The master says, "The salt is human pain. Every life has the same quantity. To surmount your pain, be a lake, not a jar." Sitting here I sense how the work creates the man, makes the Doctor himself the medicine — makes him a lake, or even an ocean.

Heart of Hearts

We've been here two hours. It's time to go. Leaving, we admire up close the giant metal heart, its left ventricle open as Dr. Evermor says hearts should be. It leans, hearts being easily pushed over. I'm still not sure what my "problem" is, but I do feel happier. The Heart of Hearts aims its love-arrow across Highway 12 at wounded Badger from some place in ourselves we long for and often sense just out of view of the roads we travel, new leaves sparking through trees as earth tilts into another spring.

V. DAYLIGHT NATION

2010-2015

SHELLS INSIDE A SHELL

I pick up half a black walnut shell. It's lain here for a season, emptied by a squirrel during the dry summer.

Its outside curvature is a shaggy ship's hull, dyed the dark black-brown of the winter sea it's about to embark on. Turning it over, I discover inside it two of the tiniest snails I've ever seen. The size of seed beads, their coiled shells are a delicate pale pink, translucent as a fingernail of the unborn.

One each clings to the walls of two grooved chambers in the walnut shell, unseen pockets of some other earth which is also our earth, where these seedling snails find protection from birds and other predators. They are so small and curled in on themselves, so much in their dream, that they bring to mind the soul washed pale and pink by the blue-black flood of oblivion in Lawrence's "Ship of Death."

Is it possible our soul is so small and delicate? Can it be that our whole life takes place inside half a walnut shell? Holding this tiny world in my hand, I feel vulnerable and unworthy. What right have I to interrupt their journey?

Carefully I turn the shell over and set it back down in the wan, late-autumn grass, where the snails' little ship can get on with its voyaging. The ragged firmament closes over them once more, their sails rosy on the hard gray waves carved inside the black walnut shell.

For Gendron Jensen

A GULL'S FEATHER

This feather is a subtle body, so light and delicate it is almost in the next life. There's a swerve or curve to the central shaft, the graceful turn of water swirling in a stream or the languid, dissipating drift of a jet trail. No color but a translucent white, through which I see the stones on which it lies near Lake Pepin, a fallen gray-blue, exiled from sky.

Maybe the soul is a single feather from some large-breasted, wide-winged bird that soars always above us.

Feather, did you fly differently as one of that brotherhood, that sisterhood, that union? What amazements did you encounter on your travels? At what point did you separate to loft away on your own? Was that what you wanted from the beginning? To be taken by the wind, to give it all up at last to air . . . To be purely conveyed, neither to resist the rocks nor be broken by them, but only to lay your sheen over them?

Unchanging, its calming olive walls and dark booths. . . . Early evening, the business rush over, almost empty. . . . I think of an old waitress who worked here . . . forever! I look up, and it's her. Glenda! Does she remember me? Probably not.

The great thing about Glenda is that she doesn't have to remember you to be instantly familiar, familial, in the Peter's manner, described by the legendary *Star Tribune* columnist Barbara Flanagan as "no-nonsense." In fact, I happen to be sitting in the official *Barbara Flanagan Booth*, dedicated in 1986. Joking, I ask Glenda what would happen if Barbara were to come in and find me in her booth. Would I get booted? Glenda replies with mild indignation, "I don't think that's likely to happen." Anyway, not to worry — Ms. Flanagan moved to Chicago and last visited Peter's a couple of years ago. "She's a very nice person," Glenda declares firmly.

Glenda's been waitressing for 45 years, and plans to cut down to part-time soon. Her doctor told her to work as long as it feels good, as he advised her during her pregnancies. "And you know what, I waitressed up until the day before I gave birth! I'd carry the tray around on top of my belly" — she rounds her arms out before her — "none of the customers seemed to mind!" She laughs fully from her thin throat.

Glenda leaves to wait on another late customer, while I write happily in Barbara Flanagan's booth. The radio plays decade-old hits that all sound slightly sad, despite their uptempo moods. I push off on that melancholy like a slow stream, amazed that this old boat of pen and paper still keeps me afloat, a child's improvisation almost, in a dark-wooded bay in one of the very best places to go in Minneapolis when you're alone.

THE GIRL WHO SANG WITH LEADBELLY

In November, 1948, someone recorded the great folksinger at a house party on the University of Minnesota campus in Minneapolis. Leadbelly is gracious throughout, the gentle giant. At the end, he even guides a very young girl through a singalong of his most famous song, "Goodnight Irene," a hit for the Weavers in 1950, six months after his death. The Weavers didn't include the "morphine" verse, but Leadbelly does in this performance. The unidentified girl's voice is small, on pitch, and piercingly high like a kitten's. It's touching to hear her hang in there so gamely with this man who once killed another in prison in self-defense, the ex-convict and the little girl singing in unison. Everything mean and hard in the man's life seems to drain away in the immense kindness of their duet. Listening, I wonder: That little girl must be in her seventies now. Was she in some way changed by singing this song, so primal it seems to have always existed, with its half-mythical author? Does she count it to her happiness and satisfaction, that bright column beside the darker column of disappointment and sorrow? Is that woman still alive? Does she still sing "Goodnight Irene"?

A DREAM OF GARRISON KEILLOR

According to my dream, he writes incessantly. We sit near each other on uncomfortable molded plastic chairs, looking out at a darkened airport runway. The night feels thick and deep. The airport bars have closed. A few lonely lights pierce the enveloping murk.

He asserts in his familiar radio voice: "It's a beautiful morning." What's this? Anyone can see it's the middle of the night. Does he have some special power to see far off where day has already broken while the rest of us sit in darkness? Or is this some sort of literary conceit?

Suddenly I realize that he is writing, testing phrases aloud as he sets them down in his notebook. Well, who knows how the dawn actually arrives? Comforted, I listen in the dead black airport night as he goes on intoning calmly: "Sun reddens the chimneys. . . . Heavy-budded trees glimmer over the rooftops. . . . Oh ever-fresh, forever lovely spring! . . . It's a beautiful morning."

THE SUPPRESSED ALBUM

Before they disbanded in 1970, the Beatles recorded a final album that was never released. *Your Peace and Mine* — with its knowing play on "your place or mine" and "peace of mind" — included a planned single, "Giant Signature," backed by "Sharecrop Summer." Ultimately, *Your Peace and Mine*, in the populist tradition of Woody Guthrie, was judged by the group's label too political, and shelved. Such secrecy was thereafter maintained that not even the most hard-core collector caught wind of the project until it was recently announced by the BBC. Pre-release publicity confirmed that Paul McCartney and Ringo Starr had gone into the studio after the holidays to augment existing tracks with a few overdubs. The surviving Beatles, along with the widows of John Lennon and George Harrison, agreed that the historical moment had arrived for the hopeful and galvanizing activism of *Your Peace and Mine.* Anticipatory tremors rocked the global media. With the album's release imminent, it appeared that the well-loved canon would have to make room for a completely new and fresh set of songs and that the Beatles would in fact change everything one more time. . . . Having now reached the end of this poem, you may understand how disappointed and robbed I felt waking from my dream, and how I regretted having to leave its reality to return to this one. . . .

SWIMMING ON LABOR DAY

Good where we've been
Good where we're going
—American Indian song

Early morning rain leaves a damp sheen on the woods. First leaf-fall like thin wet leather layers the road. Steam rises from pavement warm all night.

The beach is abandoned and calm, the outsize boats moored on the river still sleeping off their hangovers. As we wade out, minnows scatter like paint from a shaken brush. Waist-deep, I bend for an empty mussel shell shining like a silver butterfly.

It's heaven to stretch one's body within the long body of the river, to plunge hands one after the other in her substance while being held in her immense cupped hands. Heaven to feel the muscles of one's shoulders extend then contract like the mussel shell's hinge, opening and closing. Heaven to fancy one's ankles trailing off in fins. Heaven for the skin to receive the current's full-length caress, heaven for the eyes to catch the eagle flying over bright water toward water shaded by eastern hills the sun has not yet climbed.

And it is beautiful afterwards to stride dripping onto the sand, to stand here with you, my hand searching your river-slicked back for the warm place behind your heart, and to watch the hazy sun-shafts among the dark trees find trembling drops that flash gold like daytime fireflies.

The fair is over. We've grieved the passing of summer, and still the world comes to us as we move, unexpectedly, one yellow leaf, one rain-diamonded spider web, one insect hum at a time. We are still walking from the good, toward the good, one step at a time.

SYMPATHY FOR THE WASPS

The woman at the Extension office says that the two dozen or so wasps clustered under the roof eave of our porch are starving. They die off, she tells me, except for the overwintering queen who starts it all up again in the spring. They've long ago exhausted the small supply of wasp honey that fed them in the comb, and grope feebly together as though blind, searching for sugar, using up their energy reserves because it's September and the sweets of earth die back too.

In full sun they fan out on the joist, not venturing far from each other, seldom flying. Sometimes one flexes angular wings as if uncertainly testing the air, then retracts them close to its spindle body. Sometimes one looks down at me, returns my stare, antennae twitching.

At dusk, they crowd together in a tight clump to conserve heat, withdraw into a shadowy depression. By day they browse the painted wood dulled by weather, dust, accumulation of tattered spider webs, bits of captured debris. The low sun is bright and cool. The wasps are remarkably unaggressive — we have coexisted peaceably at close quarters for half a month. In warm hours a few still whirl up against the south side of the house like wild-flung honey.

BREATHE TOGETHER
November 22, 2013

> I shouted out, "Who killed the Kennedys?"
> When after all it was you and me.
> —The Rolling Stones

> You believe in redemption, don't you? —JFK

Drizzled November. Afternoon bells toll in Dallas. Crowds precipitate onto Dealey Plaza. Sorrow, shame, and confusion are not dispersed, but instead concentrated. Evil suspicions go on triangulating in the popular imagination between the School Book Depository, the grassy knoll, and the open car. We go on being perplexed. The thousands of books on JFK and the assassination only seem to push the edge of our unknowing into darker, more frightening regions. Meanwhile, the fact, sphinx-like in its sanctum, sits masked and veiled by time and plausible denial, cold and immovable as stone.

After 9/11 someone asked, "What difference in the end whether it was done by their thugs or our thugs?" I remember the shock of that. Well, what of the insistence that conspiracies *don't* occur? To whom might that be useful? Easier to accept the aberrant individual than the corrupt aggregate. Yet people do *breathe together*.

In the 1970s the Swedish poet Tranströmer joked that each person who voted for Nixon should go to jail for three minutes. Because I also long to see the guilty brought to justice, I suggest that all Americans go to jail for three minutes for killing President Kennedy. Behind bars, we could ask ourselves the question his life asked: Given the thuggishness of ourselves (which he well knew), how are we to live? We could think of him in World War II swimming those miles in the Pacific with his bad back, pulling his comrade to safety at the end of a belt clenched in his teeth. We could think of his secret letters to Khrushchev, pulling the world over nuclear waters to safe shores, where the assassins also were spared to go about their business.

A DEAD CROW

What is this basket of night dropped beside the white fence? A crow, a large one, lies on its back, stiff feet up, black claws curled, wings half-spread on the damp ground. No sign of violence — could it be that the heavy, slushy snow that breaks tree-limbs also brought down this dark neighbor during last night's storm?

There's a streaking below the anus, birdlime whiting the glossy black tail-feathers' mortal opening. Someone big has fallen out of crow-town. Eyes are closed that shared the sky with mine. And the powerful beak, matte black, sharp, gracefully sculpted . . . I bend to touch, lightly, my fingertips to its beautiful half-warm curve.

RIVER OTTER

In October the river cools and clears. Summer's algae goes the way of the other green, till all that's floating on the surface are a few late-fallen leaves, little canoes to oblivion. Mornings after the leaves are down, the river becomes a still, cold basin, misted around its shores, a bowl of quicksilver held by the frail black hands of the trees.

Looking from a bridge, you may see a dark head lifted from the water — or is it only a deadhead stump? But the stump is narrowing, turning, and finally growing more distant, leaving an oddly static white wake on the placid silence.

Look longer and you recognize the sleek muzzle, the sinuous contour of his back, diving, surfacing, undulating in and out of view, for amusement or for some more serious purpose, foraging or mating. In any case, the otter seems to prefer having the river to himself, when the migratory geese have flown off to feed in farmers' fields, leaving the morning, like the water itself, smooth, unruffled. Then he's most likely to show us his playful life, though from a distance, as if to taunt us. We imagine how the freshness of that chill immersion might yet wake us from what Frost called our "human sleep" into the otter's fluid kingdom, widening like thought in quiet moments.

KNOWING SHIT

You don't know shit. —Anonymous

Those lozenges, loaves of waste, are only the most visible evidence of the body as passage-way through which multifarious entities come and go. We know the food we eat only superficially, its inmost architectures and communities of microscopic dwellers as inscrutable to us as those within ourselves. We subsume nutrients, take them into our mysterious vitality, often without thanks, knowing neither what they are nor what we are.

At the end of the process, the dross coiled in the porcelain basin appears languid, lackluster, tired from having yielded the living energy received from soil, rain, and sun and transported to our tables in beautifully defined and varied foodstuffs, cargo ships bearing treasure from the Cathay of the world. Instead we see merely the fatigued residue of travelers exhausted by their long voyage. So spare a moment for gratitude to this unjustly maligned pilgrim, gone down to its innocent and healthful sleep in the earth, where we will someday join it.

THE MOLE

On the next-to-last day of March, I notice half-swathed in dead grass along the south side of the house a lump of velvety gray the size and shape of a small baking potato, the tail and hind legs mouse-thin.

Parting the grass bunched around it, I recognize the eye-and-ear-hidden head, the worm-like snout. Here, almost frightening — my mammal guide uses this word — are the *hands*, pink, clawed shovels wider than they are long, short-armed, stubbily attached to the upper torso for excavating.

A trail of failed burrows gouged in earth attests to a still-half-frozen garden. Upending itself in each new attempt, the mole wriggles its furry behind in air, its tiny hind feet useless while the hands scoop furiously, displacing damp black loam to either side.

Little earth-diver, the friendly waves do not open for you, and thus leave you vulnerable to larger, swifter, better-sighted predators than myself. This is the reason I tip your bumbling, blind handful into a plastic yogurt container, transport you across the street to woods margining the river. There, on a mud bank warmed by southern exposure, you paddle straight down in softer dirt, bury yourself in your element, find protection in that darkness you travel.

MARTINS FERRY, OHIO, 1987

We found James Wright's portrait there in the public library, right where "The Flying Eagles of Troop 62" said it would be. That morning in the James Wright Room I discovered and xeroxed a typed letter from 1946 written by Ralph Neal, the kindly scoutmaster praised in Wright's prose poem.

And that would have been souvenir enough, though even more memorable was the question put to me by a friendly, open-faced young man working at Di Carlo's Pizza. Taking my order for a dollar-thirty "slice with everything," the youth asked with wide-eyed curiosity, in his Ohio accent, "Are you re-LIJ-ous?"

How so?

He explained that he'd noticed me walking down Walnut Street with a book open in my hands and guessed I was an evangelist. No, I replied, just a fan stopping through to pay homage to Martins Ferry's magnificent poet James Wright.

He'd heard of James Wright, though a football player for Cleveland was the town's most famous celebrity.

As we walked out with our pizza, he blurted, "I'll probably never see you again in my life."

This boy in an earlier time might himself have been one of the scouts "that good man" Ralph Neal loved for their "scrawniness," "acne," and "fear." I said he should visit the James Wright Room and look up "The Flying Eagles of Troop 62," hoping, in what he was surely right was our one and only encounter in this life, to give him — not enough, but the best thing I could think of — the hard-won and unflinching compassion of his town's native genius.

The minister, though well-meaning, talks too much about heaven and not enough about the man who has died. My memories of my old professor are warm but sparse, giving my mind latitude to wander. I imagine the dead man asking, Did you make it to my funeral? If a person answers no, the dead man then says, OK . . . But did you make it to *my life?*

Every person in this church will have to pass through that needle's eye where my teacher has gone. That we're here this one time is all we know for certain. Shouldn't we be paying more attention to the stations of our journeying?

Suddenly I'm intensely aware of the splashy abstract stained glass, the cross embroidered on the white pall, the tall candle blazing above the casket, the hymnals' red covers, the minister saying something about "love's purest joys restored."

The honor guard files in to present a flag to the wheelchair-bound widow: A raw wakefulness stands at attention while out on the snowy church sidewalk the salute is fired and the trumpeter, a friend and retired professor himself, puts a little extra jazz curlicue on the end of *Taps*, in this daylight nation where none can keep an address for long.

In memoriam Dr. Earl Lewis

VI. BRUSHPILE SPARROWS

2016-2017

ART CAR

Driving on a gloomy, winter-worn day with gloomy thoughts, underslept, uninspired, tired in body and spirit. The freeway a succession of gray or black frost-encrusted pods hurtling and whizzing around my automotive plod. My mood brightens before, a beat later, I realize why: ahead in the right-hand lane an art car studded with small colorful objects. I step on the gas, come up alongside, see glued to trunk, roof, and hood hundreds, possibly thousands of toys and tchotchkes — dolls, trolls, smurfs, a mounted army of them, their green, orange and purple hair trailing in wind like a rainbow cotton candy comet. Plastic letters glued to the driver's door decree:

EVERY DAY IS A PARADE

EVERY DAY IS A PARADE. Do you hear that, soul? How could we have forgotten? Art car, today you alone among the enslaved multitudes catch the joyful cosmic memo of freedom. As you cut your jolly swath through the gray workaday traffic, please throw us your tow-line of color and whimsy to pull us along with you, where we all can join your diminutive marching band, streamers of bright coarse hair fluttering past our ears.

Small screens diminish the world, I think, driving my 96-year-old mother past farms near her home on a morning in what has so far proven an atypically mild November. Wooded hills and swamps alternate with fields, all harvested by now. Geese forage the corn stubble, not yet convinced it's time for them to leave. Homes variously kept up or neglected say how well, or not, each farm family is doing.

We crest a gentle rise to view clipped pastures vividly green, bordered by bristling bare trees that make a kind of spiky-hairy barrier between earth and dry blue sky. Deep in the thickets is an unperturbedness, acquiescence to what comes. My mother still knows every turn of the road — better than I do — I depend on her not to get us lost. No one complains about the weather, but there's something unsettling about this continuing moderation. This is the north country, not known for its moderation. But all that's immoderate here today is opinion. On Main Street barstool pundits badmouth Obama and agree that climate change is a leftist hoax.

I love these back roads through scrub woods that hold so much of the rugged, persistent wildness of the land in them. Since childhood they have occupied my imagination. What has happened to the imagination of others? The country is large and their world small, shrinking along with the screens. Many have never lived outside this abundance and simply can't imagine anything could threaten it.

THE HOME-GOING

I wake from a forgetting sleep a little before one, seeing with that night vision of the soul the corner of the small cemetery we approached by a narrow road winding into pines, where the old family stones, for years untended for distance and lack of nearby relatives, darken with lichen and mold. Over bare April earth we strewed the fine tan powder of her bones first lengthening in my grandmother's womb almost a century ago, matter coming home to the matter of parents, sisters, brothers, brothers-in-law, sisters-in-law.

There in that corner of the cemetery untroubled by the passage of time where two cedar trees have grown up to bracket her parents' plot, we dusted traces in loose lines no one could quite read, elemental signature of mortality soon to be scribed into ancestral ground by the force of ordinary weather.

I see it all again in the dark of our bedroom, the scrawl of ash, the gravestones, the lichen, the cedars and pines, and, superimposed on that final earth as the flickering of film on a screen, the little girl my mother was in her checked gingham, finally risen from her dolls' tea in the summer yard where a photograph held her in childhood our whole lives, now running toward the possibility of happiness that was hers from the beginning, across the shadows of this world into the waiting arms of mother and father, released from the ashes of her burned-down hopes. . . .

Born deaf, he never learned to speak, read, write, or even sign.
Apart from an unfruitful stint at a school for the deaf and blind, he
lived his 78 years surrounded by caring relatives in Boise.

He left twenty thousand drawings, many of farm scenes or enig-
matic faces. Some intriguingly include the doll-like figures his family
dubbed "friends," as though the imaginary childhood kind.

How much he made from the scarcity of his origins! He'd draw
on any available paper or cardboard, backs of envelopes, insides of
food packaging, cigarette packs, box lids, inscribing his pictures in an
ink mixed from stove soot and his own spit, his preferred medium
even when better art supplies became available to him.

Mostly gray-toned compositions, always somehow pointing back
to the dilemma of his situation, voiceless in a silent world, his art his
cry. How does one think without language? Could one deeply
apprehend without naming, so that the rendering itself became a
kind of vocabulary? He kept at it, drew nearly every day until, old,
sick, unmarried and childless, he died.

His drawings were his speech. Yet he understood that words carry
meaning, and meticulously copied letters — sometimes forming
words but often not — onto paper. It's as though an intelligent,
precocious pre-schooler had set out to write in an absence of actual
knowledge of letters. He sensed their numinosity, adored them for
their formal beauty, as perhaps we all do before we can decipher
them. . . .

And what if we could not hear human sounds and were unable
to read and write, what better solution than to draw our emotions
and purpose? What if our untrained childhood art-making, stretching
out before us, provided a road into the future? What if we'd had to
labor against frustration, to rage without music or voices through
our wholly unexplainable lifetime? In twenty thousand drawings
James Castle showed us how he lived that dilemma, with discipline,
fury, and expressive glory.

To make so much from so little — let's look in the mirror of that discipline, we who have grown complacent in making little from much.

IRISH SKIES

There's some truth in the old song, "When Irish Eyes Are Smiling." But I'm thinking this morning of a more recent song, Patrick Kavanagh's "On Raglan Road," with its "clouds over fields of May." It's May in Dublin, the robins — the small, rusty-headed ones, not our American kind — in fine voice, and the magpies performing their vivid black-and-white thieveries. And all over the generous horizon of Ireland, from mountains to the sea, sun and rain alternate, contend, debate, argue, fight, make up, and love again. I have never seen so many events occurring in one sky at the same time. To be in Ireland is to have a reserved seat in the theater of the weather. Perhaps such meteorology prepares one to live with the enlivening, changing weather of Irish eyes.

A BENCH ON THE GRAND CANAL

> O commemorate me with no hero-courageous
> Tomb — just a canal-bank seat for the passer-by.
> —Patrick Kavanagh

Our friend Tony, driving us around the even-numbered postal codes of Dublin, pulls over near the Baggot Street Bridge. We have passed the high houses of the embassies and the legendary pubs, dark and murmurous in the cultural bloodstream. Tony in his working life as a Guinness delivery man knew them all, but better yet knows which ones the poets favored.

A beautifully painted barge anchors on the beloved canal, narrow strip of water wrapping the streets with its silver ribbon.

There's a bench here we must visit, Tony explains. Two men are sitting on that bench, but only one of them is alive. That one, eating his lunchtime sandwich, graciously surrenders his place so I can pose for a moment beside John Cole's life-sized sculpture.

Ah, Kavanagh, though you're long gone from these streets of sorrow, inspiration, sickness and recovery, your form lingers as afterimage when the vision has passed — your massive metal hands, your metal hat too heavy for a mortal head to bear, as your thoughts sometimes were for you. The sculptor has rendered your face well: long, inclined toward the earth of acceptance, yet quickened with the mischief of defiance. Your body put down, your words rise up again on the wings of an obstinate joy.

In the end you asked for a bench, and here you have it, the finest any man ever sat on. And now that my friend has shared it with me, it is also mine to keep in your memory.

For Tony Condren

NEWGRANGE

The guide recommends that claustrophobes enter last, should the narrow, enclosed passage prove too intense. Cautiously, I hang toward the back as we file, about twenty of us, into the low doorway of this strangely contemporary-looking dome-like structure we glimpsed on its far green hill while approaching.

Crossing the slab threshold, edging sideways to squeeze between the massive wall rocks, I feel the numbers become physical — 5,000 years old, 280 feet in diameter, 200,000 tons of rock and earth. My discomfort slowly gives way to admiration and then to keen curiosity about the neolithic society capable of realizing such a monumental feat of engineering, a millennium before the Great Pyramid at Giza.

Sixty feet in, we crowd the inner sanctum, an uneasy roominess opening beneath the corbelled ceiling. I can't decide whether this weight I sense around and above me is of stone or time.

We know that cremated remains were brought here. Possibly the flint-hewn basins were for birthing. On sunrise at Winter Solstice light plays down the passage all the way to the inner chamber for about seventeen minutes, assuming clear weather, which in Ireland one can't. We imagine the shortest day arriving for those mysterious dwellers along the Boyne, the name by which they knew the river a part of that unraveled fabric of their lives.

The guide informs us he's switching off his lamp. Ancient darkness rushes in. We are blind in the earth. Now, slowly, electric light grows from the "roofbox" window over the entrance, lays down a ragged path, heavily shadowing the spiral incisions on walls. I hear myself letting out held breath as the weakly cheerful artificial sun relieves the tomb-darkness. It's as if a prayer has laid its light over some intractable fact of living, this pathway one of those channels prayer has carved in the human heart over thousands of years, laying luminous hands on the stones of the world.

REVISITING DARTINGTON ESTATE AFTER EIGHT YEARS

Returning weaves the familiar into the new encounter. Though I recognize the old Great Hall, the modest, functional studios, the mown grounds opening to hilly pastures of Devon, the geometrically terraced garden with trees out of Tolkien, who spent time here, I still can't recall the half of it.

What pleasure to rediscover on its chest-high pedestal the Henry Moore sculpture, an undulating woman whose simple face, shaded into the round upraised head, wears a look of peaceful melancholy. The limbs rest, almost lightly, within some unending vigilance, the mood one of elegiac repose.

Some believe that Knights Templar are buried in St. Mary's Church cemetery. A famously long-lived yew tree shadows the handful of graves. The trunk is also a sculpting, massive, slow-moving, organic, more ornately baroque than Gaudí. Literature, dance, art and thought have flowed abundantly from the human spirit in this place, but the tree was here before any of it. Christ may not yet have been born when the yew seed began its vast undertaking. The tree is known to be at least two thousand years old, making it by far the oldest living thing in my experience. I lay my hands on the knobbing, elephantine circumference that has quietly persisted in its place, and feel in my body its peculiarly deep and resonant time.

SLAPTON SANDS

Late May sunlight refracted through crystals of salt air makes for ethereal brightness. Waves from the Channel lock in to shore, shatter to hissing white lace, ocean-spread tablecloth yanked away again and again. Four adults and a child crowd by the breakwall, picking smooth stones from the wet beach, wrapped around by windy Devon coast.

In 1944, more than seven hundred Americans died offshore in a D-Day rehearsal called Exercise Tiger. A German E-boat sank them in the chill night April seas. A good Devon man, Ken Small, raised a Sherman tank from the depths to stand in memory of those forgotten dead. The wreck on its plinth across from the beach appears baked a molten black by its decades underwater, moving parts fused into a kind of giant volcanic machine fossil.

Up the beach, tourists take cream tea in a well-lit seaside B&B. Never far away, the glossy black shadow of the tank reminds us of those whom war has discomfited unto death. Meanwhile the waves keep up their liquid drumbeat, and the lacemaker-foam's hands remain busy, busy. In the midst of it all, between remembrance and the present, night-chaos and the orderly barriers of day, people on the strand huddle out of the wind, adult and child alike take in hand one pebble after another, each exquisitely sculpted, knowing the magic of peace lies in something as simple as the happiness we feel gathering beautiful stones smoothed by the sea.

For Jonny, Alice, and Aphra

THE BALLOONS

His acceptance speech delivered, the stiff, wind-swollen figure steps away from the podium into the moneyed fold of family. As if sealing the deal, the music saunters in, the Stones' "You Can't Always Get What You Want," the joke — a nasty one, on the electorate — amplifying through the hall of mirrors. The TV cameras jet back squid-like into the rafters of the convention hall for the moment of the balloon-drop, strings and clusters swirling down into the dark water of the auditorium like demon milt, turbid, cloudy, circulating dream-like on over-heated currents.

One PBS commentator remarks glazedly that she always looks forward to the balloons. The candidate may pitch xenophobia and display megalomania, but at least there are balloons. Promises to the coal industry and no mention of the environment, but at least the balloons are falling. In the darkened auditorium of the American sky, CO_2 molecules are loosed, invisible, abstract like infinitely small balloons. No wall can keep them out, along with the chaos brought not by alien agents but by the most common components of matter, the same in us all.

A BROKEN STONE

The stone has several walls, at least eight or nine depending on how you count certain angled declivities. To further confuse matters, some are dark and some are light, as if a shell or veneer of a rusty tan color has been shucked or shocked from the stone's exterior to reveal a thoroughgoing darkness.

On closer examination it's evident that the stone's interior gloom isn't unrelieved. Tiny glittering particles like sawdust or brown snow swirl the night sky of the stone. At this point the eye asks what exactly it's seeing: primordial organisms swimming in the first dark ocean? intimations of galaxies beyond counting in the farthest range of our best telescopes?

Ask instead which vision best suits the human scale. The answer: something in-between, light flecks lying upon the face of the darkness as grass seed lies scattered on black soil. As if some greenness is waiting to grow there.

Held between the thumb and fingers, the stone undergoes a miraculous transformation, as though a premonition of an entirely different existence it may know after being broken down, the ultimate end of all stone, reduced to the life-giving grains of mineral nourishment a grass-root can absorb.

To those who despair of the hardness of certain hearts and fates in the present moment, I say: One day even this stone will become a nurturer of grass.

BRUSHPILE SPARROWS

It's good to have a brushpile in your back yard. Accumulation of last year's storm-fall, it's a waist-high sheaf or wave, shapely as if composed. In mid-winter, a dozen sparrows make it their home, or if not their home, their base. In daylight one may see them clumped like thickenings of the top branches, dark beads along the curving roof beams of their stick-house. Within the snow-thatched tangle, shelter from wind and predators, shadowy flittings . . . I leave crumbs and seeds for them on a round concrete slab earmarked for a future garden project, the powder snow on top of it printed by delicate claws. Some say that God got the idea for human beings by observing birds' flight. When I approach, twelve sparrows flutter up into the black walnut tree. They make a kind of visual music, like fingers lightly brushing the strings of a harp. Watching and listening, I feel as though I'm seeing my own soul. Come spring, I'll clear it away, knowing the rain and wind will keep doing their work, and I'll begin to gather up another pile.

ABOUT THE AUTHOR

Thomas R. Smith is an internationally published poet, essayist, editor, and teacher. His first poem to be accepted by a literary magazine was a prose poem, "Ezekiel," reprinted in this volume. His work has appeared in numerous journals and anthologies in the U.S., Canada, and abroad. Garrison Keillor has featured his poetry on his national public radio show *Writer's Almanac*, and former U.S. Poet Laureate Ted Kooser has selected his poems for his syndicated column, "American Life in Poetry." He is the author of seven previous books of poems: *Keeping the Star* (New Rivers Press, 1988), *Horse of Earth* (Holy Cow! Press, 1994), *The Dark Indigo Current* (Holy Cow! Press, 2000), *Winter Hours* (Red Dragonfly Press, 2005), *Waking Before Dawn* (Red Dragonfly Press, 2007), *The Foot of the Rainbow* (Red Dragonfly Press, 2010) and *The Glory* (Red Dragonfly Press, 2015). He has also edited several books, most recently *Airmail: The Letters of Robert Bly and Tomas Tranströmer* (Graywolf Press, 2013). He teaches poetry at the Loft Literary Center in Minneapolis and posts poems and essays on his website, www.thomasrsmithpoet.com.